What Mothers Are

PHOTOGRAPHS BY LAURA STRAUS

Ariel Books

**Andrews McMeel
Publishing**

Kansas City

Photographs copyright © 2001 by Laura Straus, NY
Edited by Kelli Giammarco

ISBN: 0-7407-0548-2
Library of Congress Catalog Card Number: 00-106915

preface

*Her smooth, gentle hand caresses my brow.
I encircle her knees with my small arms, holding
tight. The folds of her skirt are pressed against my nose, cheeks, even my eyelids.
I keep my eyes shut and breathe in the warm smell of Mom.*

Photographing mothers and their children brought these memories flooding back. I found that the special bond between mother and child is palpable in a myriad of ways: in the blissful expression on Phyllis's face as she breathes in the sweet smell of Laurie's hair, in the warm embrace of Sarah's arms as she reads to Elizabeth. Then there is the vision of Mia enveloping Ashley in a fluffy towel after emerging from the sea, and of Lynn making a game of raking leaves with Christopher on a crisp fall day. There is Marilyn helping her daughter Melissa catch the high bar on the playground, and Laurie leaning toward her son Teddy while he softly kisses her forehead.

Here's to motherhood! And to each mom, my thanks for making this book possible and for allowing me to be a part of these intimate moments. Finally, to my own mother, Nina Pelikan Straus, and her mother, Vanda Pelikan, for bravely offering their hearts and their visions of the future to Rachel, Tamara, and me—the next generation—thank you.

—Laura Straus

What **Mothers** Are

your best friend

playful _____

comforting

protective _____

uplifting

good listeners _____

silly

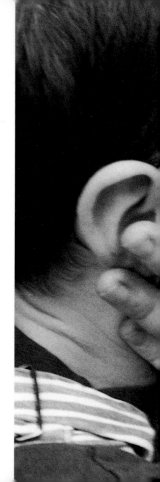

proud _____

references

beautiful _____

there to lean on

huggers

always ready to help

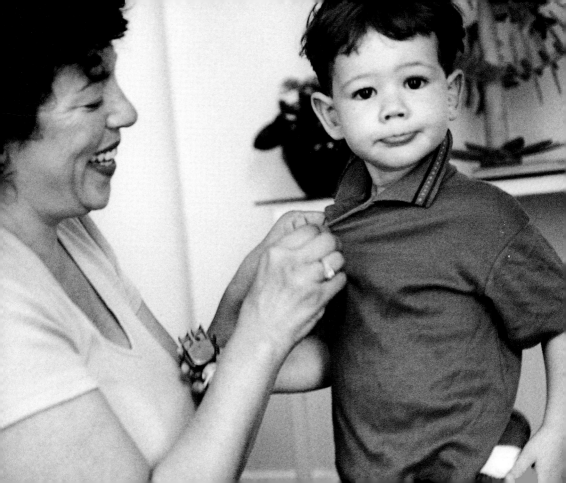

security blankets

nurturers

someone
to laugh with

rainy day company

supporting

spontaneous

playmates

full of surprises

dance partners

always within reach

the center of things

young at heart

devoted _____

one of a kind

teachers

forever maternal

your very own _____